I0616717

A Belfry of Knees

Alabama Poetry Series

General Editors: Dara Wier and Thomas Rabbitt

Alberta Turner

A Belfry
of Knees

The University of Alabama Press

WITHDRAWN
IOWA STATE UNIVERSITY
LIBRARY

Copyright © 1983 by
The University of Alabama Press
University, Alabama 35486
All rights reserved
Manufactured in the United States of America

Library of Congress Cataloging in Publication Data

Turner, Alberta T.
  A belfry of knees.

  (Alabama poetry series)
  I. Title. II. Series.
PS3570.U66B4 1983   811'.54   82-15967
ISBN 0-8173-0127-5
ISBN 0-8173-0132-1 (pbk.)

For Weese, 1889–1976

Acknowledgments

Grateful acknowledgment is made to the following publications in which some or portions of these poems have appeared:

Cleveland Poetry-in-Transit Project, 1979: "Cloth." Poetry-in-Transit was sponsored by the Poets' League of Greater Cleveland.

The Gamut: "Shetland," part 1 (no. 5, Winter 1982). In the same issue *The Gamut* also published "Brace," which first appeared in *The Whiskey Island Magazine.*

The Iowa Review: "From a Dictionary of Common Terms," parts 4, 5, and 6 (Spring 1982). First appeared in *The Iowa Review,* Volume 12, Numbers 2–3. Copyright 1982 by The University of Iowa and used with permission. Appeared again in *Extended Outlook* published by Macmillan in 1982.

The Little Magazine: "Four Fears," parts 1, 3, and 4 (entitled "Three Fears" in vol. 13, nos. 1 and 2, 1981). First published in *The Little Magazine.*

The Longman Anthology of Contemporary American Poetry: 1950–1980: "Choosing a Death." "Choosing a Death" by Alberta Turner has appeared in THE LONGMAN ANTHOLOGY OF CONTEMPORARY AMERICAN POETRY edited by Stuart Friebert and David Young, 1983. Reprinted by permission of Longman, Inc., New York.

Memphis State Review: "From a Dictionary of Common Terms," part 1 (3, Fall 1982). *Memphis State Review* © Memphis State University.

Missouri Review: "Shetland," part 2 (vol. 11, no. 1, Fall 1978, under the title "Necessary Magic"). It has also appeared in *Stand* (England) (vol. 23, no. 2, 1982).

Paintbrush: "Shetland," part 3 (vol. VI, no. 2, Spring 1979, under the title "Birthing"). "Birthing" first appeared in *Paintbrush.*

Poetry Now: "The Angel of—," part 4 (vol. IV, no. 3, issue 21); "Making Old Bones," parts 1 and 5 (vol. V, no. 2, issue 26); "Four Fears," part 2 (which was published in a slightly different form as a section of "Making Old Bones" in vol. V, no. 2, issue 26).

Quarterly West: "Shetland," parts 4 and 5 (no. 9, Spring/Summer 1979).

The Reaper: "The Angel of—," part 1 (issue 5, 1982, under the title "Reaper").

7 + 7 (1981 Prize Volume): "Knees." Copyright 1981 by the Ohio Arts Council for the Artists. "Knees" has also appeared in *Southern Poetry Review* (vol. XXII, Spring 1982).

The Whiskey Island Magazine (Cleveland State University undergraduate magazine): "Brace" and "Press" (Winter 1981). "Brace" has also appeared in *The Gamut* (no. 5, Winter 1982).

Grateful acknowledgment is also made to The Ohio Arts Council for a grant that enabled me to write a number of these poems.

Contents

I

Knees

So much to touch
I've let my fingers laze
mittened them to mere spoons
So many wires to twist and skeins to tease

So many lean things
climb   swing   hang
roll down long slopes of gravel and gorse
give birth again

And fat blunt things
used soap   used stone
chins in hands
thumbs

If Death complains
I'll say   Don't grieve
You're the drum
I thump my knee on
gong   bell   belfry
of knees

The Angel of—

"O doctor, doctor, what is your name?" "Döden."
Rilke, *The Notebooks of Malte Laurids Brigge*

1.

Something's putting on the clothes
I laid out when I went to bed
Morning runs out of the room
Have I ten toes   two ears?
Will my mouth open
to take the lip of the cream jug?

I play jokes   offer it soup
invite it in to use the toilet
draw chalk across the blackboard
to suggest a rusty scythe

(Doctor   what does this swelling mean?
"Madam   your blood will no longer run")

Sliding down the shimmer of myself
admiring the damp variety of pearl
I've made from wet sand—
Will there be cakes
on a long table and
cress with vinegar?
Perhaps not
Will raised tails run toward me?

I cup my hand under its chin for a long
look   It's crying
inside   swallowing hot salt
for some error   some red pepper
bitten too fast   I wipe sweat
from under its eyes
(I'd like it to sweat   to have eyes
I could wipe sweat from)

2.

I basket its fruit
pomegranates   mangel-wurzels
rutabagas

closet its clothes
mufflers   overalls   rows of boots
the sides slit for bunions
one three-piece suit

I walk through its house
In the kitchen coils of tubing
an outsize drainboard
In the front room too many folding chairs

Yet the house is white
and freshly planted
It improves the neighborhood

3.

First make an *O*
under that a *T*
then *A* without the brace
and flaps   dots   ends
as you please

Next give it names   pouches   spoons
its own tracks   pet tricks
then history   its acts of tenderness   wives
favorite foods

And when it's almost ready
to invite in   pretend
enemy or friend and make your own
feast of scorpions or cream
halt foot scraping or young foot springing
on stone

This your choice   him
or the slow leak   pooled grease
hanging hinge   none of them
worth keeping   or able to mend

4.

The angel of—
Everything it touches

So it tries not to touch
Gives up the tickle
of hooves in its palm
and running a wrist
down the fur of trees
When it lowers into the sea
it's careful not to reach for an island
to pull itself out

But sometimes it has to sleep
picks an empty spot
When it wakes   it forgets
stretches   and always
a silo flattened or a team
lying tangled   their necks broken

5.

I'm still not used to the idea
I'll not shake hands   I'll hover
When I go to the bathroom
I won't shut the door

It's just that I can't imagine
love coming out of my mouth
with no toothbrush in it
the chicken I ate the leg of
screaming for it back
the peas sprouting disconsolate
from my stomach

the ferry sideways in the slip

Cloth

I envy nuts   their dense flesh
I love my ears   soft   and no sound too swift
I can braid rain

Weaving sky takes most of the day

Four Fears

1.

Mostly I remember being afraid
No dark closets   no bed without supper
but pails with loose lids
caves with soft backs

Not bad now   not often
If a room is empty and the door
open   I don't wait   Nothing
taller will come through
than a large hen   tilting an eye left
an eye right   to see if I'm grain

2.

Just before waking
I'm white

Always brown in the mirror
but now white   Same features
but pale hair   pale spirals
on a cream forehead   no   not cream
white

The tall square woman
is whiter than I   wipes
paler lips   asks comfortably
if I'll hold her gloves
while she pulls her girdle down

Should be comfortable back
But I'm not

3.

A monk coughs   I clear my throat
The Good Witch says "Hold my hem
We have to swim"   I lend her my breath
In the market a root hands me a knife

They want me to ask "Mats or nets?
Stems or spines?"   Want
to dampen me with choice

Mrs. Thomas tried on the coat though
she noticed a slight movement in the sleeve

The matron put down her keys
within reach of the cage

4.

In braille feet get there first
Pavement breaks   softens
then a prostrate weed stem and a tuft
of grass   My ears comb
sparrows   ducks   a chuckle of pigeon
There must be a barn   Chain clanks down
Something pads along wood   drops

Skirt

Make a lap with no seam
stretch   but no sieve   fringe
but no broom

And deep enough to dust a hen

And flat as horizon   dry
as the sea's horizon

Making Old Bones

1.

Five barrels of flour   seventy sticks
of salted butter   Is that my measure?

Two thousand and four squeezings
of wet cloths   two thousand and eight
unwrappings of warm feet?

No matter how wide I spread
my skirt   my lap won't
hold them all

2.

Shame
airless like jello
a lemon-lime plug
in my nose   my mouth
too full to swallow

All it takes is a friend
pushing a basket through a window
across the street   the smell of rice
my child has burned   a small black Angus
shoving against the teat

3.

Too easy just to doze
without even untying my shoes
I should grate and grunt through a tight
slit   a caul of noise   bright sting   slap
Too easy this drowse   certainly false

Yet I have starved
I ate a peach thick with ants
and a hen that pulled its feathers out
and I left my teeth on a picnic cloth

Tray under washed sand
shells on cotton under glass
coffin lined   wheels oiled—

4.

There's pulse in both my feet
Her feet are numb

Hers have gangrene
but mine are warm

There's butter here if I would bake
and soap if I would carve

A young man's climbing toward me
He's my son

A young girl cries
My girl I think

She's handed me a cake
I'm squeezing it

5.

You said I'd be a good girl
if I tied my shoes   if
I'd not undress my doll
in the dining room   not
turn over the stone
to bury the worm

Here's a pill   Put it
on my tongue   Here's a paper cup
and a bent straw   Drink   Don't
wet the bed   Put in my teeth

Good

Paradise

No beak wears my hood
or nostril my ring
No mouth carries my apple to the oven

I can lie in front of a plow
and no one will catch his breath.
because he didn't see me in time

II

From a Dictionary of Common Terms

Creep

Go prone   as a serpent on his breast
a fox dragging his brush   the devil
to the table under cloth

Grow stems and branches
along the ground and underground
like cucumbers   like blood vessels
inside the womb and along the branches of horns

Grapnel dragging the bottom of the sea
small iron "dogs" braced between andirons
breed of fowls with legs so short they jump
child   too young to walk

Go on knees   or carpet   to the cross

Wear

Clothe   like the king's daughters
when they were virgins   like a necklace of garlics
or a hawk's bells   or gold in a swine's nose

Wear arms   or canes
horns   breeches   willow
brains in the belly   jewel in the forehead
sting in the tail

Destroy by use   the thresholds of rich
men's houses   the stumps of brooms
the ground by continued fruitfulness
Millstones that have worn light
must be fed slowly

Outlast   increase   "Macbriar wore down
Balm of Gilead and won by a length"
"They two women wore together for miles
wore their sheep into the fold"

Fond

Men who swear by salt   bread   fire
Hens that follow a hand for corn
Fond Ellen's child must be taught to suck

"Ritchie is fond and loves to see me fine arrayed
His finch is fond of millet seed
His brother's fond of me"

To cocker   pamper
pigeons   small cousins
"Sweet Robin" before the court

Frogs kept in glasses for fondlings and favorites
Unreasoned craving of creatures for light
Faint taste fond salt

Tis Pity

A little proud   but full of pity
for a mouth coated with flies   a foreleg held off the ground
begging (its frequency)   Christianity (its courtesy)
For pity's sake   hush

From *pietas* (duty)   extended in late Latin
to include compassion   It suits a woman
endows God with a clean mace
A pity to slaughter two that yoke so well together
A pity of his nose   he would have made a fine man else

Pleading paw   proffered cup   pitying shrug
Pitiful ships cut from paper   pitiful cookies carved from wood
I leap down   Be pitiful good Ground
God's pitikins   some fool or other knocks

Arch

Rainbow   Fountain
Bear the weight of Caesar and his triumphs
the weight of vision over the depths of error

Eyebrow   seedling   her feet
unmined remainder of a lode
vault

-bishop   -angel   -tempter   -fiend
Arch water without spilling
Arch the infinite over an apple
Overreach

Bliss

At mass   at meat
in a lusty husband's arms
of a child in her grace
Bliss on bliss

Felicity   ignorance
what the Pope has not got

A bliss of birds
a bliss of *yes*

Bliss   obsolete of *bless*

Die

In harness   in bed with your shoes on
at the stake   in your mother's lap

A calf   by witchcraft
A new child   by fondling

Lakes die   and barbarian nations
intricate vices   lard lamps   red trout
A good death   an utter death   die out

Forgive

Soft word   softer than *lean* or *yield*

Forgive me my trespass through your sweet peas
forgive my eating your cold blue plums and using your comb
My dent in your mattress is much like yours

Ask and you shall be . . .   You admit the fault?
Go on   cut a sneer in my pumpkin
make a little catskin muff out of my pet
pay me on the courthouse lawn

•

A woman forgave her husband
propped notes on his coffee cup   taped one
to his gardening shoe   even hired a blimp
to stream FORGIVEN across the sun
When he begged   screamed to know why
she scratched in dust on his dresser
"Darling I could forgive you anything"
When he moped   she squeezed his hand
"It's all right Love   you're forgiven"
And when the letter bomb came through the slot
she called "Stay there Hon   I forgive you"
and opened it

•

Sand dunes on the Magdalen Islands
are clay bluffs the sea forgave

A mouse   cornered   reared on its hind legs
and bared its teeth   The cat was shocked
but forgiving

Horses forgive their dung

●

In a barn with no windows a Houyhnhnm keeps the insane
He comes from a race of cloudless minds
but these are all hoof and canter and floating tail
So he fills their house with bells and funny forests
and fat foals on wheels   And every ten feet
he hangs baskets of grain just the height of a nose
Tails are unbraided and manes grow long
Only a few neigh and paw the walls
for pardon

●

"Pardon   where is the Ladies Room?"

"Pardon   but if the hair is thick and smooth
thorns are the only crown that will stay on"

"Pardon Madam—   This way Madam—   Pardon"

●

Forgive me

Good

A squat jug?
A mongoloid that sucks its thumb
and offers me a suck?

Perhaps a pair of thick hips?
A chair that has a cushion and a back
but no seat?

Something's threading double-camels
squinting   squeezing   tugging at their lips

Something's loose among the basins
tubs and bins   of tubers   stolons
corms and buttons   shrapnel   gears   and cuffs

I'm not sleepy   I'm not sad
I'm not wet   I don't hurt
I'm not glad

Gold? Chick? Food?

Your toes test the tub   your thumbs dot
the edges of knives   One hand takes the handle
the other lifts the spout

You draw water from a well with a heavy lid
lift it   close your eyes   dip your pail
You won't look down and risk a frog

Why not?

When a hole takes your hand   you risk coin
When a dog wags its tail   you ignore the growl
And you know a valley has no shade at noon

Dust is for rolling kittens
Pumpkin blooms are to fry
And consider the sun   hitching a chariot
dressing up like Louis XIV

Consider the hen—

Smoke

Saints curl like smoke from stone
a loaf like any   no stake nor sticks
only the hump   and the humped shade
of rock   Strong tang of burn   a nodding
toward each other   they spiral off

Child   who watch and eat an onion now
and fold your legs and worry
saints have been making here so long
they layer   Their weight ignites

Weight will shell you out and strike you
on yourself   Stone and the weight
of stone   smoke enough

Keeping

In this frame a clock is keeping and a hunted man
and a wheel of cheese   A kept woman keeps
circling   They keep distance   silence
balance   a painter's keeping

At the edge a daughter is let out   weeping
She carries a small fish on her palm   "Daughters
and dead fish are not for keeping"

•

Suppose you play hide-and-seek and outrun
the count of ten and crawl under a root
and the others give up and you wait and fall
asleep and night and rain and the root
keep you and you forget   Suppose ants and sun
Suppose a dog smells you and calls and they call
him off   Suppose a rockslide or a mudslide
or a parking lot—

•

Tip the bag and shake the angels out
They flutter   blink   wing-stagger up
One at the bottom's limp
Wingtip to wingtip   at arm's length
you carry it to the trees and throw it in

Where did you bag those angels and what for?
Were they heaped in the orchard stung by bees
or spread across the well top soaked with sun
or perched in a row on the clothesline you reeled in
dazed from feeding in the mulberry tree
their white   asleep   so bright
you had to keep them?

•

Dream   and the ears come off
Look   and the cheek smears
Touch   and you erase

Lightly Stranger   Lightly Earth—

Leosan

From *los*   *ruin*
of current by reduction of voltage   of soldiers
by injury or capture   Puzzled
perplexed   not able to   uncertain how

Cheap   below cost
not to be found   no longer held
parted from in a crowd   having wandered from
having no sense of shame   scattered by Assyrians

Four pairs of shoes   all of them walked
a raincoat   hung by its chain
a pitcher of dimes   two hotel soaps

No thing wasted
Leosan   *los*

Knowing

Cattle are dropping   horses have purple tongues
and geese hatch with the wings on backward
Their child was born with one kidney   Her teeth
are brown and shaped like rabbit ears   They know this

•

If I saw myself walk in   I wouldn't know
her   If she took the deep chair and pulled her
short legs up and tucked them under and opened her
bag and pulled out paper and a black pen and
pulled the top off with her teeth and dropped
the pen and hunted in the crack beside the cushion
and found it on the floor and if she wrote and
scratched it out and wrote it over and scratched
it out and bit the pen and if it were June and
then October and she wrote again in the deep chair
with the black pen   my name   I wouldn't know
her   I would not know her

•

Painting the steps
alphabetizing the herbs
counting all the winter caps
and pulled scarves
we look up
A far stump splits a rock
We leap the crack

Backed against wood
slipping our shoulders up onto smooth
hooks   pressing till the spread prongs
clamp our wrists   jabbing our feet down
down for the iron socks
we lift

Some of us are close enough to knowing
One hand with three fingers
to feel for the other seven   two hams
to inch across the room   and perfectly
matched eyes

•

The deaf juggler lays three balls on the table
then two more   tosses them to make sure
spaces them an inch apart   then fills a cup
with water and puts it in their reach
Next he climbs onto the bed and faces the door
He knows he is their anteroom   He will know if they call

Truth

A shimmer a quiver on skin or linen
an opal set in a toad's face

I squeeze whatever squeezes and may be food
I peel whatever sticks

A white eye is an oiled hand is an apron
is a bell

And you who are right and know it
square your chin at me   through milk

Drift

Imagine bouncing   bumping   humping over a cliff
the briskets heaving   the baskets hooping   the birds inside out
Imagine settling out of the high air
loops   beaks   tiny dolls with inch-long skirts

Then imagine rain   The draggle of it
glinting mud   drying paste
one doll's skirt over its head
the feathers stuck   their quills all whichways

and wind   winds

III

Thread

The dead are away from home   A truck drives up and men in uniform unscrew the house numbers and disconnect the phone One brings out a quart of milk   one a pitcher of goldfish A child unbuckles the collar of the hound chained to the porch   A neighbor cuts lilacs and leaves a note   Two passersby unhook the clothesline and count the pins   And an officer carts a freezer to the curb and takes the door off The last one out   a woman   carries a jar of screws and a box of threads across the street   "The Byrnes are dead" she explains   "Will you keep these for them?   No one can say when they'll be home"

Before Meat

Child   don't forget your top
The dog will be boiled by tomorrow night
Don't go farther than the trees
until he catches up

Keep an eye on our door   The hall light
will be on till the sun comes up
You can't get lost   It's like a vacuum cleaner
with a high sweet hum

When you come to a river bribe
a goat   or while the bull's busy
climb under him   You'll find you can
swim   Though the shore is glass
the next wave will slap you up

Legend talks of passports   Otomé offered
hay   You can wiggle your ears
If the guard has three heads   remember
one is horn   one beak   only one
is tooth

On the ninth night I shall break
fast   offer you turkey
in a small pot with a hole
in the bottom   In the morning
the house will be swept
for the first time

The Prudence of Nan Corbett

I didn't know which would work   so I tried
them all   Savings and Loan   Savings and Trust
early Mass   salt over my shoulder   In spring
I poured cider on the plow

But winter came anyhow
A hare sucked my cow dry   my hens got roup
my fur went bald   my battery died

This year I really tried
I asked for Gene at the Full Service Island
butchered the pig in the waxing moon
and when a black dog tried to lead me home
with him I threw a bone in front of the dog

But winter came
My feet went through the Chevy's floor
I forgot to tell the bees and they swarmed away
I got the roup   my tractor lamed

So much for luck   Next year I'll make sure
have my spleen and my appendix out
spit twice when I harness a white horse
rustproof the Chevy   and on Christmas Eve
I'll spread fresh straw   shut the stable door
and won't look

The Devil

While his crib still had sides   he woke screaming
arms beating   as if he'd been dropped

Found it easy to bite off
stems   bits of skin   spit them out
But numbers came wrong   Three apples
take away three left three cores

When he blew on a grass blade
no one came   When he caught a finch
he squeezed too hard

He enjoyed fire   Ears wrinkled   hair hissed
But his own finger hurt

Old Clootie   Teaser   Lad
Lurk in a pocket   lurk behind the Cross
take the hindmost   beat your wife
behind the door with a leg of lamb

Your special shoes   your forked sock
Your bedpost   paintbrush   darning needle   apron
your young   your milk

And all you know of falling is that dream

Short Commons

Bloated with hunger we enter Hunger's village
It squats   a slack pouch   and we question it
"Are you made of skin?   Were you once fat?
do you wear a hunger belt?"

In the breeding zoo the female gorilla
lifts her infant's huge and puckered
head like a curious melon

In the art museum a blind boy touches Venus
"A nude!" He laughs from lobe to instep
instep to lobe

White celery   square carrot   pigmy
Someone told moss it's a bed not a stand of spruce
Cattle for slaughter are kept in the pining house
"Christ minds only to diet   not hunger you"

Shetland

1.

Stone tunnel where a Stone Age man
crouched from stone bed to stone hearth   Stone
stack where a bishop laird stored his bells his cannons
flutes and casks   Seven long concrete sheds
where cattle stand from calf to beef
their dung on a slide-out tray   their hay
in a moving trough

2.

In Shetland they don't name the dead
say "her that were tint
them that's awa
the bairn I wanted"

When gravediggers find a lamb
in the churchyard a child will die
The lamb will have three legs

When a small pig runs begging
they dig where it wants and find
a child secretly buried

The beds they die on are burned
If smoke from the "leek straw"
blows over a house a child will sicken

When they build a church
they bury a live
lamb under it

3.

The cock crowed at midnight
but a rainbow arched over the crib

Crossed signals
Have I rocked an empty cradle
carried fire out of the house?

The priest would say "God's will"
The doctor "Keep warm"
They do what they can

I must borrow a black cock
take the knife and the Bible to bed
and talk to this child

4.

"Give us"
(This day?
I asked for sun   but my well's dry)

"Don't give then
and don't take away"
(Ice on the watering trough?)

"Take then
and give what You can   Can You lend your bull?
I'll work him till You come for dung again
and I'll keep the calf   one of the calves"

5.

Backs of trucks hunching over rock
down to a quay   mailboat nosing in
cattle bunched to board   a flock of sheep
their long ears back like rabbits   and a dog
weaving the air shut behind them

Three Easters

Walking a cliff with a lamb
in my arms   the ewe stumbling
and chattering and looking up

Climbing down
the lamb in a sling   the ewe
calling from the beach

Standing on deck
squeezing the lamb to stop our shivering
a rumor of ewe   a rumor
of shore   in mist

IV

Brace

Take an island so small that when you look up
sea's every *thing* and every *where*
Gulls cruise the edges   feet tucked up
clams burrow and squirt
your feet soak

You turn and climb   Sand slurs a track
stacked holes are cities of rabbits
splashed stones guard eggs   and someone has wrecked
a small plane

Inland and up   through alder and tamped bracken
Someone is wintering sheep here   They scatter
then bunch and wait   You climb
they bolt

Rock now and lichen   then a pool
rimmed with reeds   snail shells   mouse traces
You stop

But wind drags past you   towing sand   towing salt
your hair   your coat   You look up
and there's the sea

Press

Grieve away and back
circle   turn it over   move the legs
try to move the legs   brush off flies
bring a box   line with grass   press the grass
add clover   press the clover   bring a shovel
ladle it in   curl the tail in with a stick
press down the lid   get a rubber band
get another rubber band   dig   dig again
dig deeper than you need

In Love with Wholes

1.

You crawl around a rim
hold grass by its flat sides
find stones with hollows for your knees
drink only on clear days when blue
falls into pools   What do you mean?

You mean   but right and wrong don't form
Just beads on string   Some are blank
Some have faces but you can't arrange them
Some are soft and won't come off
Cut the string   and someone else strings

Moles burrow blind   Wings fold frayed
You bed on old burrs with soft prongs
They find you smoothed and bury you
in an egg   What have you said?

2.

In love with wholes you round the heel
toward the toe   knit two together
down to one   cut thread
hide the end
                 Or you pull your skin
over your head and ease out the arms

The jar you placed in Tennessee
tilts and fills with rain   You try
a castle   it doesn't speak
A flagpole takes five men to heave it up
You stand upon that hill and turn
North beetles   East stares   South yawns

Then wings pin your arms
                              "You write death"

Not really   A moleskin
makes a doll's rug   half a day
covers a well   my aunt's black stole
shows birds where corn is sown
                              "Show birds and you starve
                                        a farm"

Not really   Birds drop some

3.

Air from the north so clear
you can see a boat beach on a cloud
You follow men from that boat up a cliff
toward a fire and its cave
You breathe   lean   listen   thin   steam

But you're not gone   That's it
You're not gone

Clenching

To want to cry and want so much not
to cry   for half a moth   a goat whose forelegs
wouldn't work   Jimenez' swollen burro and the child
who rode him in her fever with such laughter
Long after their graves are grass
I slap them from my mouth

•

Calf with a ring in its nose
battering a fence to tell it horns
Mouse belled with a cat's bell
though it hangs too low on a mouse
to give tongue
Sand swirling a swale no water will use
burying an arm to uncover an arm
Note for the milkman   head in the oven
Fist falling asleep   and dropping you

•

Poll   geld   spay
dock   crop   shear
fleece   flense   flay

and stand   now
in the whole stare

Choosing a Death

1.

It's I found the iron kettle
my choice to fill it
If it empties on my foot
if I cook a friend
my choice too

Nothing happens
the curtains straight   hollyhocks
waiting for frost
Blood moves so slow even reeds don't lean
So I need to make a gate   no knotholes
a waterfall on this side
and over the top twigs or a bulbous cloud

Or the maid's room in your house Weese
white iron bed   white spread
dry January flies
cracks between the boards (lemon)
stairs down to the kitchen (clove)
since your stroke   no sheets

Spit into the wind   and camphor balls
glass bells   salt flakes   Spit again
and every size glove   Cough
and jacks you can count with a red ball

Outside there's nothing to do
So I shut my eyes and wait
for snow hiss on teasel or
trickle down pine   I know
blood settles into sludge   You
felt your pulse   Mother
asked for breakfast   I
walk along a shelf   push
every bottle off

Superstitious? Of course
I raise my eyes to three soft candles
and I'm three
The street is cobble   the priest and saint
up ahead   chanting
I scuff in petals and coffee grounds
over my shoes   "Shame   bad"
You laugh and pull me back
But lying on my back   the warm wet
disgrace halfway to my waist
the blanket drawn up
I like that

The stalk that rain pushed down
turns up   but only at the tip
and come an east wind what about
pines bent only from the west
or the fat drop
in rain?

I'm afraid
I lean down and tie my shoe
But my sore throat is mine

And then outside a theater its picture
on tiptoe holding me straight up   my tutu
a stiff wing   laughing over its shoulder
at me in the rumble seat   curving
down from the trapeze to catch
my hands   pleading with me
from behind bars
Its face folds to the woman's
in the change booth
She is old and whimpers when I pull
the nipple from her gums
She grows small in my arms   I fold
the corner of the blanket over
her head

I wear a charm around my neck
The chin is almost worn away
I fold my thumb into my palm
lift it to my mouth

2.

It plays cards in a tavern with three men
and mentions buried gold
It sits on a rock combing its hair
slips off and comes up under my boat
Through the planks I feel its playful butt
It floats by on a log
On the bank grass slants and trees lean
sun moves up or down   I have been and am
going to be   Do I really want
that rose explosion?
Back in the tavern one asks to be dummy
and leaves the room

In my fever I go looking for my death
It will have shape and weight
will come in a mason jar or hang
from a ring   If I pull and it snaps back
it may be mine   or if it bounces
higher than my hand   It won't
be a fistful of rubber crumbs

I walk into the shoe-repair shop
It's over thirty days but I have a ticket
Someone burrows in the back   I hear
the click of heels   the plop
of rubber soles   and his muffled
"Will you please come and look"

Or I look for a long horse   one of a row
tied to a rail   I walk slowly
behind them   One slaps its tail
and shifts weight   One twitches
off a fly   Hobson says "Take the first one
They're all the same"
He's lying

Or I find a fan   Ease right and the thin bones
slide apart   precise   overlapping   the veins of ribbon
taut   It's a wing folded   Folded how long?
How do I know the ribbon's young?
The ring in my hand is green
If I leave it folded it still looks strong

In the drawer all the underwear is dry
Blood and milk have been soaped
and squeezed   elastic relaxed
the snags ironed and pulled through
Dark and camphor   I feel too good to move

Tell me   is this the way to . . .
                              "How much rice in your
                                           pocket?
                              Have you told birds?"
In the sky   clouds petal   and repetal
around a mouth

My brother was cut from that funnel womb
an arm at a time   To be I had to lift
the whole roof   but the roof's silted shut
and the way back will be an arm at a time

Are you my death?
                                        "I'm your earring"
Have you got it under your arm?
                                        "That's my kidney machine"

Phoenix   phoenix
who's got the phoenix?

3.

Mueng Lin chose plum blossoms and river mist
one man with his one ox
and a wicker basket that might hold fish
Made a bet with himself   if the man were at least
seventy and if the sun had just set or the man
had just napped   he'd take whatever that man caught
and put in his basket

I slide in through a tube and walk around
Rails   a curving bed of Queen Anne's lace
Tracks I suppose
as if I were a crossing-keeper's lodge
the sunflowers and poppies growing in cinders
and edged with whitewashed stones   as if
the train would come

One of them will have warm flanks   a nibbling lip
a jingle of bells in the pasture   snort
when it comes toward me   nuzzle my pocket
I'll mount and trot in a soft thud of peat
and ammonia steam   dip under an apple tree
pull one off
One is loose just behind the rim of trees
I hold out sugar   trip over a vine
and pull myself down   When I sit up
I don't feel like riding

A horse less in the stall   the smell
of urine almost gone
Billy stamps in the next box
then walks out   holding his bit
bright with his own saliva   arching his neck

Did I say *death?*   I'm not sure it was
not even sure anyone rode out
now the manure's dried

                              "Do you need a death?"

Yes Weese   I need one

                              "Why?"

Suppose there were no traffic lights
and no exit signs and no speed limit
and no rest stops and . . .

                              "You don't believe that"

But the caterpillars are woollier
and the acorns have thicker shells

                              "They always do"

I *need* to pretend water   pretend feed
prop the door open a crack . . .

                              "Stop this foolishness
                              and run along"

But gravity's no pun
The mercury won't fall below the glass
And I'm used to lying still
while zero jumps up and down
And when I wasn't looking
you came Weese   And just before you left
your arms   my hands   your scratchy face . . .
                              "What can you make?"

Woollier for one
ears so tall a whole herd
can winter under them
a horse that . . .
                              "Choose then"